Pen to Paper

Tricia Hedge

Nelson

Thomas Nelson and Sons Ltd
Nelson House   Mayfield Road
Walton-on-Thames   Surrey KT12 5PL

51 York Place
Edinburgh EH1 3JD

Thomas Nelson (Hong Kong) Ltd
Toppan Building 10/F
22A Westlands Road
Quarry Bay   Hong Kong

© Tricia Hedge 1983

First published by Thomas Nelson and Sons Ltd 1983

ISBN 0-17-555394-7

NPN 19 18 17 16 15 14 13 12

Printed in Hong Kong

Acknowledgements

Illustrations
Cover by Dan Pearce
pp.18 and 20 Julia Whatley
p.30 Nigel Paige

Photographs
The publishers would like to thank the following for their
kind permission to reproduce copyright material:
pp.9(top left and bottom left), 27 and 56 S E Hemmings
p.12 Character Cottages Ltd
p.15 Corfu Villas Ltd
p.32 Press Association
p.37 British Tourist Authority
pp.42(top right) and 54(top left) David Simson
pp.42(bottom left) and 43 Keystone Press Agency
pp.42(bottom right) and 54(all except top left) Val Wilmer
p.61 Jenny Mathews

Texts
We are grateful to the Youth Hostels Association, England
and Wales for permission to reproduce (adapted) copyright
material on pages 28 and 29.

Contents

Introduction to the teacher

Pen to Paper is the first book in the Skill of Writing series. It is primarily intended for teenagers and young adults, but has also proved successful with older students. *Pen to Paper* is a supplementary book designed for students with one year's (60–90 hours) English competence. Its main objective is to develop the writing skills but, as a structurally graded book, it also consolidates students' growing knowledge of English and develops a wider range of vocabulary. Teachers can use the book at intervals throughout the year, either in the order of units given, or as the topics, structures or vocabulary presented here integrate successfully with the mainstream course. The book consists of twelve units, each with a minimum of two hours' work, and a Consolidation Section which usually offers a further task for homework.

Structures

Pen to Paper is structurally graded and is based on Stages One and Two of *English Grammatical Structure* by Alexander, Stannard Allen, Close and O'Neill (Longman 1975). The structures are introduced progressively, reinforcing those commonly found in the first and second years of a general English course, and they are practised within the context of a particular writing purpose, (for example, adverbials for describing daily activities) and always in a natural context of language use. A detailed structure list for each unit follows this introduction.

Vocabulary

It is not possible to produce a supplementary book which is appropriate to the grading of vocabulary in all mainstream courses. Vocabulary development, therefore, is an important aim of *Pen to Paper*. The vocabulary arises from topics and the Consolidation Section at the back of the book contains a vocabulary list for each unit. Vocabulary is carefully contextualised through pictures and texts so that the meaning of a new word is easily understood.

The Writing Tasks

Pen to Paper contains many different types of writing for a range of purposes, for example, writing letters, instructions, dialogues and a review. Dialogue has been included because, although not a natural form of writing, except in literary contexts, it is a task often set in public examinations and students need practice from an early stage. Simple compositions have also been included as these often form an important part of English assessment in many educational institutions. By working with different writing purposes students can learn how these require different styles and how to use the appropriate language.

The Approach to Writing

Each unit guides students towards a final piece of writing through careful preparation of subject matter and through detailed language practice. On the one hand a topic and its relevant vocabulary are introduced and the students are required to gather information concerning the topic. On the other hand students are given practice at the different levels of language: structural, organisational (the clear handling of content in a logical order), functional (such as using the best linking devices to create coherent writing), and stylistic (using vocabulary appropriate to context). A clear context in each unit ensures that students understand the nature and the purpose of the writing task.

The Units

Each unit follows the natural steps in constructing a text: finding words, linking ideas, making sentences, organising the text; though the order of these may change according to the type of text. Students follow section headings which make clear the nature of the activity.

The emphasis in *Pen to Paper* is on expressing information in a logical order in clear simple English. The book tries to give an increasing degree of freedom in both the form and the content of the writing. It encourages students to work creatively with English by gathering and using information in different ways and by drawing on their own knowledge of the language. Each unit contains activities which range across the language skills: speaking, thinking, finding out, listening and reading. Since writing in real life is associated with experiences in these skills and usually derives from them, the writing tasks in *Pen to Paper* draw on what students do and learn in other activities.

Using the Book in Class

The book is designed mainly for use in a classroom with the guidance of a teacher who can exploit the possibilities for pair and group work. The teacher can also encourage students to work together in groups to check and revise each other's work before presenting a final version. Alternatively, many exercises and activities can be done individually either in the class or at home, especially the Consolidation task, so that students can apply the skills they have learnt to the writing of a similar text. An answer section at the back of the book provides the key to closed exercises, that is, those which have only one possible answer.

Although the Skill of Writing can be treated as a series, no one book is dependent on another, therefore *Pen to Paper* can be used as a work complete in itself, and no reference to any of the other books is necessary.

Structures used in each unit

1 Everyone likes him!
Present simple tense of verbs, including *be*
Third person 's' in present simple
Adjectival phrases after the noun phrase, e.g. *with fair hair, with blue eyes*
Simple adjectives to describe people, e.g. *tall, short, thin*
Adverb of frequency: *usually*

2 Is it near the sea?
Present simple tense of verbs
There is/there are/there are lots of . . .
It is/it has . . .
Adjectival phrases after the noun phrase, e.g. *with a garden*
Simple adjectives to describe places, e.g. *comfortable, sunny*

3 He never gets up early
Present simple tense of verbs
Adverbs of frequency: *never, sometimes, often, always, rarely*
Adverbial phrases of time: *in the summer*
in the winter
on weekday evenings
on Saturday evenings
on Sunday mornings

4 Come to my party!
Prepositions of place, e.g. *across, along, over*
Imperatives for giving directions, e.g. *go along, turn right*

5 Are you a new student?
Present simple tense of verbs
Present continuous tense of verbs
WH interrogatives with *what* and *where* in present tenses
Connective: *because* with clauses of reason

6 Don't leave anything behind!
Imperatives for requests and orders, e.g. *please don't . . .*
Verbs which take infinitives:
help to   remember to   forget to

Modal verb: *you must/you mustn't*

Describing a person

UNIT ONE
Everyone likes him!

Finding Words

1 Think about a person you like. Describe him or her. Write five sentences.

Is he/she tall?
Is he/she thin?
What colour are his/her eyes?
What sort of hair has he/she got?
What sort of clothes does he/she wear?
What sort of person is he/she?

This is Chris, Jenny's boyfriend. Jenny is writing to her friend, Barbara, about him.

He's very tall and quite slim, with dark, curly hair and brown eyes. He usually wears casual clothes. He likes wearing jeans and a denim jacket. He's a serious person, quiet and gentle but sometimes he's very funny. Everyone likes him because he's so kind

2 Which words describe Chris? Make lists. Then write down the words about your friend from Exercise 1.

Looks	Clothes	Personality
tall		serious

Learning New Words

3 Work in a group. Read out the sentences about your friend. Listen to the sentences from students in your group. Write down new words you hear in your lists.

4 Look at the notes about Barry and Angela. Make notes about John and Penny.

BARRY

Looks: *very tall, thin*
short, straight, fair hair
blue eyes
Clothes: *casual*
checked shirts, jeans

Personality: *honest*

ANGELA

Looks: *quite short, slim*
short, fair, wavy hair
green eyes
Clothes: *fashionable*
dresses, jackets

Personality: *sympathetic*

JOHN

Looks:
Clothes:
Personality:

PENNY

Looks:
Clothes:
Personality:

5   Look at this sentence.

He's a *serious* person, *quiet* and *gentle* but sometimes he's very *funny*.

Choose the best word to describe these people. Write the number in the box.

| i easy-going | ii | ambitious | iii quiet |
| iv cheerful | | v sympathetic | |

a) ☐ Barry wants to be a director. He works very hard.

b) ☐ Penny is always smiling and happy.

c) ☐ Angela likes to help her friends. She listens to people's problems.

d) ☐ Chris doesn't talk much. He likes to think.

e) ☐ John works with little children. He's never tired or angry.

Making Sentences

6   Look at this sentence.

He's very tall and quite slim with dark, curly hair and brown eyes.

Write four sentences.

Barry   He's very tall and thin with _____
Angela   She's quite short and _____
John   He's _____
Penny   _____

7   Look at these sentences.

He usually wears casual clothes.
He likes wearing jeans and a denim shirt.

Write four sentences.

Barry   He usually _____
Angela   She _____
John   _____
Penny   _____

Organising Your Writing

8 Now write about this girl.

a) She's _____ with _____ and _____
b) She usually wears _____
c) She likes _____
d) She's a _____ person, _____ but _____
e) Everyone likes her _____

Writing It Out

9 Make notes about a person you know.

Notes
Looks
Clothes
Personality

Now write out a description.

10 Write a description of someone in your class. Read it out but don't tell the other students the name. Can they tell who it is?

UNIT TWO
Is it near the sea?

BOVEY
Cottage for 4

Large, _____, detached 15th century cottage with thatched roof, in small village next to pub and church. Rose garden around cottage with _____ patio. Large, beautifully furnished living room with 2 _____ sofas, pretty windows and _____ wood fire. _____ kitchen with breakfast corner. Two bedrooms, one with double bed and one with two _____ beds. Bathroom and w.c.

Two miles to shops at Moreton. Many _____ houses and gardens nearby. Fishing in River Bovey. Horse-riding in village. Quiet country park with swimming pool 2 miles. Sea 5 miles. Very good for picnics and touring.

Services.
Central heating, _____ TV, payphone, garage.

Weekly Rents

Jan 3 -Feb 21	Feb 28 -Apr 4	Apr 11 -May 16	May 23 -Jul 4	Jul 11 -Aug 29	Sep 5 -Sep 26	Oct 3 -Oct 24	Oct 31 -Dec 12	Dec 19 -Dec 26
£ 84	117	142	155	175	155	117	–	–

Finding Words

1   Read the text. Complete it with these words.

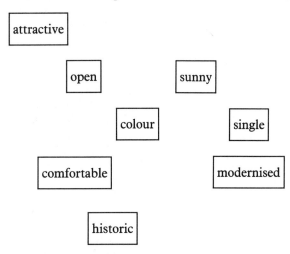

attractive

open   sunny

colour   single

comfortable   modernised

historic

Learning New Words

2   Look at these words from the text.
    Which is the right meaning for each one?

cottage	eating outside on a trip
patio	made of dried straw
detached	a place to sit in the garden
picnic	small house in the country
thatched	not joined to another

Making Sentences

3   Which sentences are true? Correct the false ones.

   a) It's three miles to the shops.
   b) There are three bedrooms in the cottage.
   c) The cottage is in a large village.
   d) There are two comfortable armchairs in the living room.
   e) The cottage is next to a pub and a church.
   f) There is a swimming pool two miles away.
   g) There is an electric fire in the living room.
   h) The living room is small.

4   Work with a friend. Ask and answer.
    a) How many people is it for?
    b) How many bedrooms are there?
    c) What is the kitchen like?
    d) Is there a big living room?
    e) How is it heated?
    f) Has it got a garden?
    g) Is there a telephone?
    h) Is it near to the sea?
    i) Can we park the car there?
    j) What can we do around there?

5   Tony and Sue are talking about the cottage. Sue is looking at the brochure and
    Tony is asking questions. Complete their conversation.

Tony   Remember we need a cottage for four: you, me, your sister and John.
           How many bedrooms are there?
Sue
Tony   And is there a big living room we can sit in?
Sue
Tony   What about cooking?
Sue
Tony   I need a telephone. Is there one?
Sue
Tony   Can we park the car there?
Sue
Tony   John likes swimming. Is there somewhere he can swim?
Sue
Tony   And what about a pub for me?
Sue
Tony   Ah well, it sounds very good. Let's phone them and book it.

6   Look at these sentences:

There is a pub in the village, next to the church.

There are lots of shops at Moreton.

Now make six true sentences from this table.

There	is are	a garage a swimming pool two single beds pretty windows a payphone lots of places to see	two miles away in one bedroom next to the cottage in the living room in the cottage nearby

7 Look at these sentences:

It's a fifteenth century cottage *with* a thatched roof.

It's a detached cottage *with* a pretty garden.

Now match something from A with something from B and complete the sentences below.

A	B
quiet park small village large living room modernised kitchen rose garden	pub sunny patio swimming pool two comfortable sofas breakfast corner

a) Two miles away there's a country park. It's a _____ with a _____
b) The cottage is in the village. It's a _____
c) Next to the living room there's a kitchen. It's _____
d) The collage has a small garden. It's _____
e) There's a living room _____

Organising Your Writing

8 Write Sue's letter to her friend Pamela.

For example:
cottage: It's a fifteenth century cottage with a thatched roof.

cottage >

village >

garden >

living room >

bedrooms >

area >

things to do >

We're going to a cottage in the west of England for two weeks. It's a fifteenth century cottage with a thatched roof. It's in a small _____

There _____

There _____

The cottage has _____

There are lots of _____

We can _____
It's very good for _____
I'm looking forward to it. Write and tell me about your holiday.

Writing It Out   9   Look at this description of Villa Mariana in Tuscany. You are going on holiday there. Write a letter to a friend about it.

VILLA MARIANI
PETRASANTA, TUSCANY

For 6 persons

Living/dining room, kitchen. Four bedrooms (2 double, 2 single), bathroom, shower room. Balcony, patio and small garden with barbecue. Private parking, 1350 metres from the beach.

A lovely villa, near to local shops and restaurants. Comfortable, furnished in modern Italian style. Large modern kitchen. Cycling, sailing, horse-riding, tennis nearby. Good for quiet evenings after sunny days. Day trips to Pisa and Florence.

UNIT THREE
He never gets up early

Finding Words   1   English people often do these things in their spare time:

go to the cinema
visit friends
watch TV
go for a walk
watch football
read a newspaper

Which things do you do? Write down some more things you do.

2   Work in a group. Ask and answer.

What do you do in your spare time?
– I go to the cinema, I visit friends _____

Listen to your friends. Write down the new things in your list.

3 Now choose things from your list. Write eight true sentences about yourself.

   a) I never _____ in the summer. *play card*
   b) I sometimes _____ on Saturday evenings. *go to moves*
   c) I often _____ on Sunday mornings. *get up late*
   d) I always _____ in the winter. *stay home*
   e) I rarely _____ on weekday evenings. *go dacning*
   f) I sometimes _____ on Saturday afternoons. *go shopping*
   g) I always _____ on Sundays.
   h) I often _____ on weekday evenings. *watch television* *review new work*

Making Sentences

4 Work with two friends. Ask and answer. Write notes about your friends in the table.

   What do you do on Saturday evenings?
   – I sometimes go to the cinema.
   – I often go to a party.

	marcela 1	shilpa 2
On Saturday evenings: sometimes often	*go visit my friends* *watch T.V*	*watch TV.* *sew*
On Sunday mornings: never rarely	*go to work.* *go to the chuck*	*go to temple* *library*
On weekday evenings: always never	*learn English* *knit*	

5 Now think of five questions to ask your friends. Write them down, like this:

   Do you ever go to a party on weekday evenings?
   Do you ever play football in winter?
   Do you ever go skiing in the summer?
   Do you ever _____?

   Ask your friends these questions and make notes of their answers.

6 Now write eight true sentences about one of your friends. Remember 's' on the verb.

   a) He/she sometimes visits friends on Sunday mornings.
   b) He/she _____

7 Look at this information about the Clark family.

never	rarely	sometimes	often	always

horse riding — *take a day for a walk* — *goes sailing*

in the summer

| Geoffrey | Stephen | Tina | Mrs Clark | Mr Clark |

go fishing — *go skiing*

in the winter

| Stephen | Tina | Mrs Clark | Mr Clark | Geoffrey |

theatre — *play darts*

on Saturday evenings

| Tina | Mrs Clark | Mr Clark | Geoffrey | Stephen |

on Sunday mornings

| Mrs Clark | Mr Clark | Geoffrey | Stephen | Tina |

go out

on weekday evenings

| Mr Clark | Geoffrey | Tina | Stephen | Mrs Clark |

plays. records,

Are these sentences true or false? Correct the false ones.

a) Geoffrey never goes skiing in the summer.
b) Mr Clark often reads a book on weekday evenings.
c) Stephen often goes fishing in the winter.
d) Mr Clark never goes sailing in the summer.
e) Tina sometimes goes to the cinema on Saturday evenings.
f) Stephen rarely plays football in the summer.

8   Make the questions. You can see the answers.

a) When _does_? he go to the pub on Saturday evenings.
   He goes to the pub on Saturday evenings.
b) How _often_ does she listen to records on weekday evening.
   She sometimes listens to records on weekday evenings.
c) What _does_? she do on Saturday morning / she go for a walk.
   She goes for a walk.
d) Does _she_? play tennis on Sunday mornings.
   No, she never plays tennis on Sunday mornings.
e) How often _does_? she do ski? in the winter.
   Sometimes in the winter.
f) What does _she_? do on Friday evenings / listen to records.
   She always listens to records.

9   Work in pairs. Ask and answer. Like this:

Does Mrs Clark play tennis on Sunday mornings?
– No, she doesn't. She never _____

Does Tina go riding in the summer?
– Yes, she does. She sometimes goes riding _____

Organising Your Writing

10   Complete this description of Sandie. Think of things to write about her.

In the summer Sandie sometimes _____ . She rarely _____ television but she sometimes listens to _____ . In the winter she _____ goes skating. She never _____ swimming. It's too cold. She often stays _____ and reads a _____ . On Saturday evenings she _____ . She never _____ at home. On Sunday mornings she sometimes _____ with her brothers. On weekday evenings she reads a book or sometimes she _____

Writing It Out

11   Now write a description of one of your friends.
Write about his or her activities, in the summer, in the winter, on Saturday evenings, on Sunday mornings, on weekday evenings.

19

UNIT FOUR
Come to my party!

Finding Words

1 Write down the names of these places and things.

Learning New Words

2 Put these words in the right lists on the next page.

football pitch   art gallery   newsagent's
bus station   swimming pool   museum
theatre   car park   greengrocer's
hospital   butcher's   sports hall
post office   garage   bank
cinema   school   baker's
club

Transport	Culture	Services	Shops	Entertainment/ Sport
railway station bus station	library art gallery museum	church school café hospital post office car park garage bank	supermarket butcher's newsagent's greengrocer's baker's	pub football pitch swimming pool sports hall theatre cinema club

Making Sentences

3 Work with a friend.
Look at the map. Ask for and give directions.
You are at The Green Man.

Can you tell me the way to the school, please?

– Yes. *Go across* the road and *along* The Green *until you get to* Pope Lane. *Turn right* and *go along* Pope Lane and *over the bridge. Turn left* by the church *into* Westfield Road and the school is *on the left.*

Ask for and give directions to:
Old Hall Farm
Finstock Health Centre
Finstock Sports Club
Manor Farm

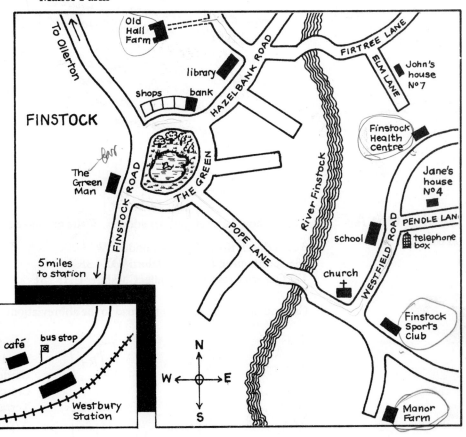

4   Look at the map again. Complete Jane's letter with these words:

to	from	around
next to	at	along
on	by	into
opposite	over	in

4, Pendle Lane,
Finstock,
Ollerton,
Herts.
OL6 4RT

June 6th

Dear Julie,
It's my birthday next Saturday. Can you come to a party? It starts at four o'clock in the afternoon.
You can get a bus _to_ Finstock _from_ Westbury Station. The bus stop is _at_ the station _next to_ a café. Take a number 5 bus to Ollerton and get off _at_ a pub called The Green Man _in_ Finstock.
Cross the road, walk _around_ the pond, turn right _into_ Pope Lane and walk _along_ the lane and _over_ the bridge till you get to the church. Turn left _by_ the church and go along Westfield Road. Opposite the school there is a telephone box. Turn right into Pendle Lane. Our house is _on_ the left. It has a red door.
I hope you can come.
                    love
                    Jane

Setting Out An Address

5   Look at how Jane sets out her address. Write out these addresses.

3 Silverbirch Road/ Ealing/ London/ W13
138 Westbourne Avenue/ Oxford/ OX4 3RZ
171 Queens Crescent/ Cheadle/ Cheshire/ CH3 2SJ

6   Can you match the name of the road to the abbreviation?

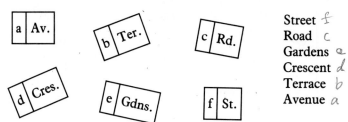

a	Av.
b	Ter.
c	Rd.
d	Cres.
e	Gdns.
f	St.

Street f
Road c
Gardens e
Crescent d
Terrace b
Avenue a

Organising Your Writing

7 Look at the map. John lives at 7, Elm Lane. He's having a party. What directions must he give to his friends? Put these instructions in the right order. Number them 1 to 7.

| 3 | Walk along until you get to the library. |

| 2 | Walk around the pond to Hazelbank Road. |

| 1 | Get off the bus at The Green Man. |

| 6 | Turn right into Elm Lane. |

| 4 | Turn right into Firtree Lane. |

| 7 | Number 7 is on the left. |

| 5 | Go over the bridge. |

8 Here is the invitation. Now write John's letter to his friend Tom. Write the address first.

John invites you to a party
at 7, Elm Lane
on Saturday 9th July
at 7 p.m.

R.S.V.P.

Dear Tom,
I'm having a party next Saturday.
Can you come?

Writing a dialogue

UNIT FIVE
Are you a new student?

1 Look at the poster and answer these questions:

   a) Do you think a fresher is:
        a full-time student?
        a second year student?
        a part-time student?
        a foreign student?
        a new student?
   b) When is the market?
   c) What can you get there?
   d) What can you do there?
   e) Where is it?

SALTMARSH COLLEGE OF HIGHER EDUCATION

FRESHERS' MARKET

Tuesday September 29th
3–6 p.m.
Assembly Hall
North Building

All new students are welcome.
Join the Students' Union!
Get your discount railcard!
   (full-time students only)
Get your disc for the carpark!
Make some friends!

Join a club!
Mountaineering Club
Swimming Club
Tennis Club
Science Society

Industrial Society
Athletics Association
Photography Club
Music Society

Making Sentences

2 At the market Ana, from Bolivia, meets Chris, from Greece. She wants to be friendly. What questions can she ask him? Write the questions.

Name	What's _____ ?
Country	Where _____ ?
Home	Where _____ ?
Work/study	What _____ ?

What else can she ask?

Do you like _____ ?

Are you interested in _____ ?

Have you got _____ ?

Working With Sentences

3 Write the dialogue between Ana and Chris. Choose sentences from the boxes and finish the conversation.

ANA	CHRIS
Are you interested in climbing?	Yes, I think so.
Do you like working there?	Yes, because the people are friendly but I want to speak English, not Greek.
Yes, I am. I'm doing Secretarial Studies full time. I want to be a bilingual secretary. I'm from Bolivia. Where do you come from?	Yes, I'm studying English. I'm a part-time student. Are you a new student too?
Have you got a job?	It's OK but I want to go to London next year.
Hello, it's very crowded in here. Are you a new student?	Greece.
Let's join the Mountaineering Club.	Yes, I work in the Acropolis Restaurant on the Broadway.
Do you like Newfield?	

Ana	Hello _____ ?
Chris	_____ ?
Ana	Yes, I am _____ ?
Chris	_____
Ana	Have _____ ?
Chris	_____
Ana	Do _____ ?
Chris	Yes, _____
Ana	Do _____ ?
Chris	_____
Ana	Are _____ ?
Chris	Yes, _____
Ana	_____

Chris and Ana meet other students. Look at this information about them.

Student	Study	Subject	Ambition	Feelings about work/study
Pierre	new F/T	Economics	to help his country	interesting
Winston	2nd year F/T	Hotel and Catering	to go to Jamaica and manage a hotel	hard but practical satisfying
Kerri	new P/T	Business Studies / works as a clerk	to get a good job	useful course people in office friendly
John	2nd year P/T	Tourism / works in travel agency	to travel	likes meeting people at work
Helen	new F/T	Photography	to work for a big magazine	creative

(F/T – full-time; P/T – part-time)

4   Complete these dialogues.

a)   **Chris**   Are you a new student?
     Pierre   Yes, _____ . I'm studying _____
     Chris   I think Economics is hard. Do you like it?
     Pierre   Yes, because _____ and I want to study it because _____
     Chris   Are you interested in visiting British factories?
     Pierre   Yes.
     Chris   Let's join the _____

b)   **Ana**   What _____?
     Winston Hotel and Catering. I want _____
     Ana   Do you like studying?
     Winston Yes, because _____

c)   **Chris**   Where _____?
     Helen   Hong Kong.
     Chris   Are you _____?
     Helen   Yes, I'm a new full-time student. I'm _____
     Chris   Why are you studying _____?
     Helen   Because _____

d)   **Ana**   Do _____?
     John   Yes. I work in a travel agency three days a week and I study _____ the other two days.
     Ana   Do you like your job?
     John   _____

e) | **Chris** | Are you a new student? |
    | **Kerri** | _____ |
    | **Chris** | Have you got a job too? |
    | **Kerri** | Yes, _____ |
    | **Chris** | Do _____? |
    | **Kerri** | Yes, the people in my office are friendly. |
    | **Chris** | Do you like swimming? |
    | **Kerri** | Yes, let's join _____ |

Organising Your Writing

Look at this information about Maria.

NAME *Maria Martelli*

AGE *18*

NATIONALITY *Italian*

COUNTRY OF ORIGIN *Italy*

ADDRESS IN ENGLAND
*141 Edgerton Street
Newfield*

STUDY/WORK DETAILS *part-time student of English
assistant in Health Food Shop*

AMBITION *to study Medicine at university
in Italy*

FEELINGS ABOUT WORK/STUDY *friendly people
learn about food*

INTERESTS *swimming, tennis*

Writing It Out

5 Write a dialogue between Chris and Maria.

Chris	Hello, are you a new student?
Maria	Yes, _____
Chris	Why are you studying English?
Maria	Because _____
Chris	Have you _____?
Maria	Yes, I work _____
Chris	_____?
Maria	Yes, the people _____ and _____
Chris	Are you _____?
Maria	_____

UNIT SIX
Don't leave anything behind!

Learning New Words

1 Complete the text from the brochure with these words.

dormitories   *kitchen*   *rules*
hosteller   *meals*   *simple*
housework   *member*   *warden*

Youth Hostelling

Y HA

Do you want a cheap and comfortable holiday with lots of young people to meet? Come Youth Hostelling. Youth Hostels are _____, comfortable houses. They are cheap and friendly. Young people can stay in Youth Hostels all over the world. Most countries have hostels. There are nearly 300 hostels in England and Wales, with another 150 in Scotland and Ireland, 3000 on the continent and hundreds in other countries from Iceland to Japan. Anyone over five can be a _____ of the Youth Hostels Association.

In a hostel you can find _____ for men and women, washrooms, a common room. Sometimes you can eat _____ in the hostel and sometimes you can cook in the _____. There is a _____ in each hostel who looks after everything. And every hosteller must obey the _____.

Every _____ helps with the _____.

2 Work with a friend. Ask and answer.

a) What is a Youth Hostel?
b) How old must a member be?
c) Where can you find a Youth Hostel?
d) What can you find in a hostel?
e) Can you eat in a hostel?
f) What must every hosteller do?

28

Making Sentences

3 Here are some notices from a hostel. Make rules. Look at this example.

| LIGHTS OUT 22·45 | You must put the lights out at 22.45. |

| NO FOOD IN THE DORMITORIES | You mustn't bring food into the dormitories. |

Make a rule for each notice. Use these verbs with *must* or *mustn't*.

bring   smoke   make a noise
drink   go into
be quiet   come in

4 Mr Fordham is the warden of a large hostel. He is making a notice for his hostellers. It's a list of rules. He is writing it in easy English because some of his hostellers can't read English very well.

Look at this text from the handbook and complete the rules for Youth Hostels in England and Wales.

Rules for our members

1. Hostels are closed every day between 10.00 and 17.00. The warden does not always answer the telephone during the day.

2. Hostellers must give their membership cards to the warden and write their names in the housebook.

3. All hostellers must do simple housework, for example, washing up and peeling potatoes.

4. All hostellers must use a clean sheet sleeping bag. The hostel rents these to hostellers.

PLEASE REMEMBER

1 Don't arrive ___ the hostel between ___

2 Make sure you leave ___ before ___ in the morning

3 Remember to give ___

4 You must do ___

5 Always use ___
  You can ___

29

5 Match each picture to a rule. Write the letter from the rule next to the picture.

a) Please try not to waste food.
b) Don't leave anything behind!
c) Please don't talk for hours on the telephone.
d) Make sure you are using your sleeping bag correctly.
e) Change your shoes inside the hostel!

Pauline is staying at a Youth Hostel. Look at part of her letter.

> The hostels are very comfortable. I enjoy meeting lots of young people and the wardens are friendly.
>
> There aren't too many rules. We make our beds in the morning and we keep the dormitory tidy. The dormitories are very clean. We mustn't keep food in them and we mustn't smoke in them. And, of course, we must be quiet after Lights Out at 22.45.
>
> We have some housework every day. I help to set the tables for breakfast and clear the tables and wash up after breakfast.
> We went to a dance last night and we were late back. The hostel closes at 10.30. The warden was

Can you finish the last sentence?

Writing It Out 6 Find information in the letter to complete the warden's rules.

```
6 Please remember to ——

7 Always ——

8 Don't ——

9 You mustn't ——

10 Please ——

11 Please help to ——

12 Always ——

13 Don't forget to ——

                              Maf Fordman
                                 3/3/83
```

Note: The information in this unit may not apply to Youth Hostels outside England and Wales.

Writing a report

UNIT SEVEN
West Africa welcomes the Pope

Finding Words

Tony James is a newspaper reporter. Read his notes about the Pope's visit.

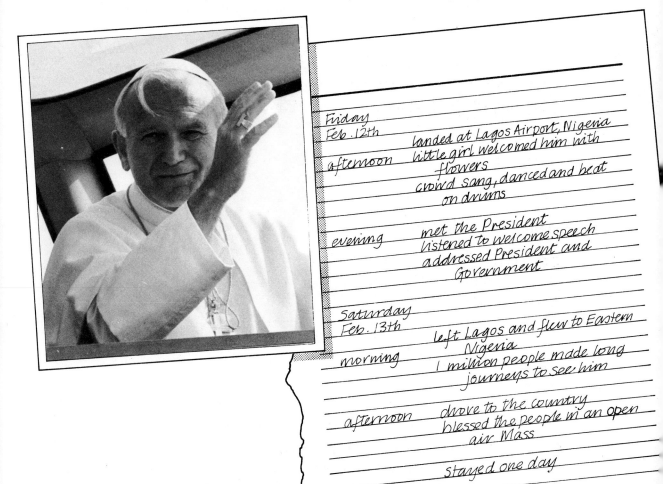

Friday
Feb. 12th
    landed at Lagos Airport, Nigeria
afternoon little girl welcomed him with
        flowers
        crowd sang, danced and beat
        on drums

evening met the President
        listened to welcome speech
        addressed President and
        Government

Saturday
Feb. 13th
    left Lagos and flew to Eastern
    Nigeria
morning 1 million people made long
        journeys to see him

afternoon drove to the country
        blessed the people in an open
        air Mass

        stayed one day

1 Make a list of the verbs in the notes. Write them in two columns. Like this:

regular	irregular
landed	sang
welcomed	

2 Work with a friend. Ask and answer.

When did the Pope land in Nigeria?
– On _____
Did he arrive in the morning?
– No, in _____
When did he address the President?
– In _____
What did he do the next day?
– He _____
Did he bless the people?
– Yes, in _____

3 Read this text from Tony's report. Write in the verbs from your list on page 32.

New Catholics greet the Pope

**from our correspondent
in Libreville, Tony James**

On the morning of 17 February the Pope _____ Lagos and _____ a short visit to Benin. Benin is a small, French speaking country west of Nigeria. President Kerekou _____ him at the airport and the Pope _____ to a twenty-five minute welcome speech.

Then the Pope _____ to Libreville in Gabon. Crowds of people _____ and _____ along the route from the airport to the city. The Pope _____ in an open car and _____ the people along the road. Military helicopters _____ above him. In Gabon he _____ in a small house on the hillside by the Sainte Marie Cathedral.

4 Are these sentences true or false? Correct the false ones.

a) On 17 February the Pope flew east from Lagos.
b) The Pope stayed in Benin for two days.
c) President Kerekou welcomed the Pope at Libreville airport.
d) The Pope drove from Libreville Airport to the city in an open car.
e) He stayed in a house near the Sainte Marie Cathedral.

5 Now complete this.

_____ Friday 12 February the Pope arrived _____ Lagos Airport _____ Nigeria. He landed _____ the afternoon. A Nigerian girl welcomed him with flowers, and a large crowd sang and danced. In _____ _____ the Pope addressed the President and the Government. The _____ day he flew _____ Eastern Nigeria and blessed the people in an open air Mass. He stayed there _____ _____ _____ .

33

Making Sentences

6 What did the Pope do next?
Rearrange the words to make complete sentences.

---

	flew/east/of/the/to/Kaduna/Nigeria/the/from/Pope
14 February	at/he/and/five hundred thousand/people/him/Kaduna/welcomed/landed
	priests/ordained/an/in/open-air/Mass/he/ninety-three
	asked/he/for/Christians/Muslims/and/between/love
	brought/fruit/people/honey/the/altar/to/and
	sermon/finished/he/his/from/with/words/language/the/Hausa

Write out your sentences like this:

a) The Pope _____
b) He _____ him.
c) He ordained _____
d) He _____ Muslims.
e) People _____ altar.
f) _____ finished _____ language.

Organising Your Writing

7 Here are some events from the Pope's visit. Put them in the right order. Number them 1–8.

| | He addressed the President and the Government of Nigeria. |

| | The Pope ordained ninety-three priests at Kaduna in Northern Nigeria. |

| | He held an open-air Mass and one million people came to see him. |

| | The Pope landed at Lagos airport and a little Nigerian girl welcomed him with flowers. |

| | The Pope visited Libreville in Gabon and drove in an open car from the airport to the city. |

| | The Pope flew to Eastern Nigeria. |

| | He asked for love between Christians and Muslims. |

| | Crowds of people sang and danced along the road. |

34

Writing It Out

8 Now write a report of the Pope's visit with the sentences from Exercise 7. Put these at the beginning of sentences.

On Friday 12 February	In his sermon
In the evening	Three days later
The next day	On 14 February
In the afternoon	

WEST AFRICA WELCOMES THE POPE

from our correspondent in Lagos

On Friday 12 February

Crowds of people sang and danced along the road.

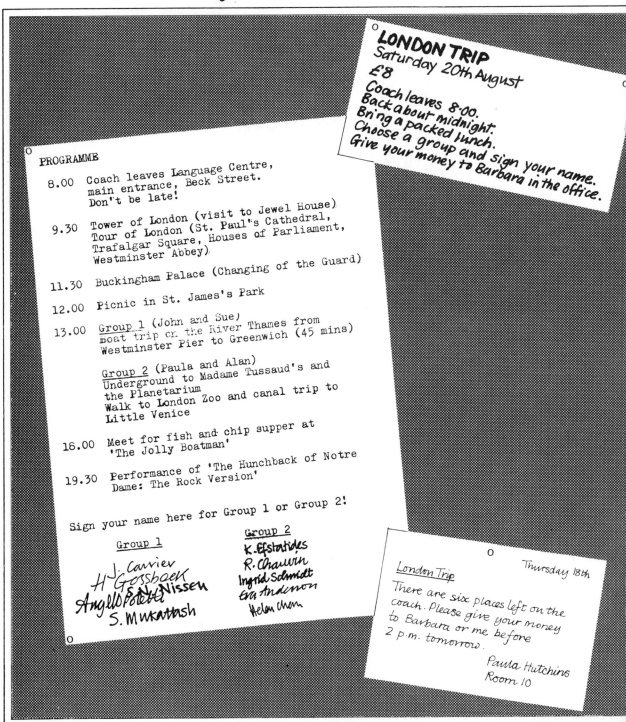

LONDON TRIP
Saturday 20th August
£8
Coach leaves 8·00.
Back about midnight.
Bring a packed lunch.
Choose a group and sign your name.
Give your money to Barbara in the office.

PROGRAMME

8.00   Coach leaves Language Centre, main entrance, Beck Street. Don't be late!

9.30   Tower of London (visit to Jewel House) Tour of London (St. Paul's Cathedral, Trafalgar Square, Houses of Parliament, Westminster Abbey)

11.30   Buckingham Palace (Changing of the Guard)

12.00   Picnic in St. James's Park

13.00   Group 1 (John and Sue) boat trip on the River Thames from Westminster Pier to Greenwich (45 mins)

      Group 2 (Paula and Alan) Underground to Madame Tussaud's and the Planetarium Walk to London Zoo and canal trip to Little Venice

16.00   Meet for fish and chip supper at 'The Jolly Boatman'

19.30   Performance of 'The Hunchback of Notre Dame: The Rock Version'

Sign your name here for Group 1 or Group 2!

Group 1
J. Carrier
H. Gossbaek
S.N. Nissen
Angello Potebl
S. Mukattash

Group 2
K. Efstatides
R. Chauvin
Ingrid Schmidt
Eva Anderson
Helen Chen

London Trip   Thursday 18th

There are six places left on the coach. Please give your money to Barbara or me before 2 p.m. tomorrow.

Paula Hutchins
Room 10

Madame Tussaud's

Home of the oldest and largest Waxworks in the world, Madame Tussaud's is open every day from 10.00 am to 6.00 pm (including Sundays and Bank Holidays).

London Planetarium

An experience in space and time! Performances every hour, on the hour, 11.00 am to 6.00 pm, on Sunday 1.00 pm to 6.00 pm.

Greenwich

Boats leave Westminster Pier every 20 minutes from 10.00 am. Adults: £1.90 return, £1.30 single. Children: £1.00 return, 75p single. The National Maritime Museum is open from 10.00 am to 6.00 pm, Sundays 2.30 pm to 6.00 pm.

Getting back from Greenwich: Bus 53 to central London, or to New Cross, then Underground. British Rail from Maze Hill or Blackheath.

The Cutty Sark is a famous clipper built for the Far East tea trade, now a museum. The hold and the crew's quarters are open to the public.

The London Zoo in Regent's Park houses the most comprehensive collection of animals in the world. Open 9.00 am to 6.00 pm in summer, (Sunday and Bank Holidays to 7.00 pm), 10.00 am to 5.00 pm in winter.
Aquarium and Children's Zoo included.

Learning New Words

1   Look at the information about the London trip. Complete this conversation.

Ingrid	Look! There's a _____ to London.
Angelo	When is it? Mm, _____ _____ August. I'm free then. _____ you?
Ingrid	Yes, let's go. How _____ is it?
Angelo	Eight pounds. I can afford it. _____ you?
Ingrid	Yes, I think so. Look, in the programme it says there are _____ _____ . Which one are you interested in?
Angelo	Let's see. The _____ trip. I like boats. _____ you?
Ingrid	No, I _____, but I like animals. I want to go to _____ _____ and Madame Tussaud's. My sister went there last summer. It's very good.
Angelo	Okay! Let's _____ our names on the list.

2   Find this information and make notes about:

The trip
When is the trip?
Who must students give their money to?
How much does it cost?   £8

The programme
When does the coach leave?   8.00 am
Where does it leave from?
What time is the Changing of the Guard at
     Buckingham Palace?
What time does the evening performance begin?

The people
Who likes boats?
What does Ingrid want to do?
Who is organising the trip?
Who are the leaders of Group 2?

The places
How long does the Thames boat trip take?
What is the Cutty Sark?
Which museum is at Greenwich?
When is Madame Tussaud's open?
How often is there a performance at the Planetarium?

Working With Sentences

3 Look at Angelo's account of his day out. Are the sentences true or false? Correct the false ones.

> a) The coach left at 8 o'clock.
>
> b) It took an hour to get to London.
>
> c) We went to the Tower of London and looked at the Crown Jewels.
>
> d) The coach drove us around the town.
>
> e) We saw the Changing of the Guard at Buckingham Palace at 11 o'clock.
>
> f) For lunch we had a picnic in the park.
>
> g) I went to Greenwich on the Underground.
>
> h) I saw an interesting museum and an old sailing ship.
>
> i) We met the other group at 6·30 for supper.
>
> j) We saw a performance of the rock version of 'The Hunchback of Notre Dame'.

4 Where can you put these sentences in the story?

> I took some photographs of the soldiers.
>
> Heinz and I went on board to look around.
>
> It took 45 minutes on the river.
>
> We travelled back by bus and underground.
>
> I almost missed it!

5 Now write out the story. Use these:

First of all _____
Next _____
At 11.30 _____
Then _____
In the afternoon _____
After that _____
In the evening _____

Angelo and Ingrid are talking on Saturday evening.

Angelo   Did you have a good time?
Ingrid   Yes, it was fantastic! Madame Tussaud's was very crowded. We waited
half an hour to go in. But the waxworks were very good. And the
Planetarium was like a journey in a spaceship.
Angelo   Did you go to the zoo?
Ingrid   Yes, we walked across the park and, after the zoo, we went on the
canal in a boat.
Angelo   You said you didn't like boats!

Writing It Out

6   Ingrid wrote about her day in her diary . Write out the diary in full sentences, also
using the information from the dialogue above. Use these:

First of all _____
Next _____
At _____ o'clock _____
Then _____
In the afternoon _____
After that _____
In the evening _____

Start like this:

'I met Heinz outside the Language Centre at 8 o'clock. Angelo was late _____'

SATURDAY 20 AUGUST

Met Heinz outside Language Centre - Angelo late! Arrived Tower of London 9.30 - saw Crown Jewels - very beautiful.

Coach tour round London - saw St. Paul's Cathedral, Houses of Parliament etc - saw Changing of Guard - took photos - Lunch in St. James's Park.

Afternoon - Visited Madame Tussaud's & Planetarium - very good . walked to zoo - went on canal trip .

Had supper at Jolly Boatman. Saw evening performance of rock show.

UNIT NINE
I prefer Biology to Maths

Learning New Words

1   Stephen is writing to his penfriend, Enrico. Look at part of his letter. Complete it with

     and   *but*   *because*

I am a student at a Sixth Form College. All the students here are between sixteen and nineteen years old. I am studying Music, English Literature and French ____ I do some Maths and Biology too.

I like my main subjects ____ I don't like Maths. It's very difficult ____ I'm very bad at it. My teacher says I'm careless. I'm taking Maths ____ I want to go to university or Music College ____ I must have a science subject. I prefer Biology to Maths ____ we do some interesting field studies. English Literature is interesting. We have a good teacher ____ I enjoy reading novels and poetry. In French I like literature better than language.

Music is my favourite subject. My music tutor is very intelligent and kind. I want to be a musician ____ I play the piano, guitar and cello very well ____ music is very important to me.

I belong to our college Community Work Group. We do a lot of different things on Saturdays and in the evenings. Sometimes we take handicapped children on trips, sometimes we visit old people ____ sometimes we help to paint their houses. I prefer visiting to painting.

2   Complete these sentences with *and*, *but* or *because*.

   a) I enjoy English. It's interesting _____ I'm very good at it.
   b) Sometimes we play football on Saturdays _____ sometimes we go swimming.
   c) David wants to study Medicine _____ he isn't good at Biology.
   d) Those two students play the piano and the guitar _____ they can't sing.
   e) Maria is studying Zoology and Chemistry _____ she wants to be a doctor.
   f) Carlos helps his father in the garage _____ he doesn't enjoy it.
   g) I prefer Biology to Maths _____ Maths is very difficult.
   h) He enjoys studying English _____ he doesn't like German.

3 Complete each sentence with an adjective. Write the number in the box.

i	main

ii	difficult

iii	bad

a) ☐ My teacher helps me a lot. She is very _____
b) ☐ Biology is _____ to me because I want to be a doctor.
c) ☐ I can't understand it. It's very _____
d) ☐ Carmen is _____ at languages but
e) ☐ she's _____ at science subjects.
f) ☐ Tony's _____ subjects are French and English but he studies Spanish too.
g) ☐ I like History better than all the other lessons. It's my _____ subject.
h) ☐ You must try not to be _____ in the Chemistry laboratory.
i) ☐ I like Biology. We do _____ field studies.

iv	careless

v	interesting

vi	good

vii	favourite

viii	kind

ix	important

Making Sentences

4 Look at these patterns from Stephen's letter.

I like my main subjects *but I don't like* Maths.
I prefer Biology *to* Maths.
I like literature *better than* language.

Choose pairs and make six sentences. Use each pattern twice.

tennis	Physics	Cookery	classical music

Italian	pop music	football	the cello	German

the guitar	Chemistry	Woodwork

5 Look at what Stephen says.

go to college
study Music
read novels and poetry
play the piano
do interesting field studies
visit old people
take children on trips

I like going to College. I enjoy studying Music and reading novels and poetry. I like playing the piano. I enjoy doing interesting field studies. I like visiting old people and I enjoy taking children on trips.

Make a list of things you do.

Say what you enjoy or like doing.

41

6 Look at this sentence from Stephen's letter.

I want to be a musician *because* I play the guitar, piano and cello very well, and music is very important to me.

What do these people say? Write five sentences.

Karl-Heinz
interpreter,
good at languages

Ingrid
nurse,
wants to help people

Rosa
surgeon,
good at science subjects

Luigi
pop star,
likes singing,
good at music

Philip
carpenter,
good at woodwork

7 Look at this part of the letter again.

'I belong to our college Community Work Group. We do lots of different things on Saturdays and in the evenings. Sometimes we take handicapped children on trips, sometimes we visit old people . . .'

Do you belong to something? Write three sentences.

What do you belong to	I belong to _____
When do you meet?	We _____
What do you do?	Sometimes _____

Organising Your Writing

8   Here is some information about Enrico. Complete the sentences.

College	Technical High School
Main subjects	Mechanics, Technical Drawing, Maths
Other subjects	Chemistry, English
Interests	Football Club, Radio Society

a) I am _____
b) My _____
c) I do _____
d) I belong _____

9   You are Enrico. You are writing a letter to Stephen. Look at these questions first. Use the information above. Think of some answers yourself.

a) Where do you go to school?
b) What are your main subjects?
c) What other subjects do you study?
d) Which subjects do you like?
e) Which subjects are you good at?
f) Which subjects don't you like? Why?
g) Which is your favourite subject?
h) Do you have good teachers?
i) What do you want to be? Why?
j) What do you belong to?
k) When do you meet?
l) What do you do?

Writing It Out

10   Write Enrico's letter. Start like this:

> 3 via de Santa Melania,
> 00743 Roma
>
> Dear Stephen,
>
> Thank you for your letter. I enjoyed reading about your studies. I think I told you in my last letter, I am a student too. I go to ...

UNIT TEN
The Secret of Five Chimneys

Work with a friend. Ask and answer.

How often do you read a book?
Do you prefer fiction or non-fiction?
Are you reading a book at the moment?
Is it a good book?

Learning New Words

1 Do you know the names of different types of books? Write an example of each type.

Type	Example
a biography	
a science fiction book	
a love story	
a historical novel	
a detective story	
a thriller	
a mystery story	

2 Sally is reading a book called *The Secret of Five Chimneys*.

THE SECRET OF FIVE CHIMNEYS
Donald Murray

Do you think it is: a war book?
a love story?
a mystery story?
a travel book?

Making Sentences

3   Read this conversation.

Tim	What are you reading?
Sally	It's called *The Secret of Five Chimneys*. It's by Donald Murray.
Tim	What type of book is it?
Sally	A mystery story.
Tim	Is it good?
Sally	Yes, it's very good. It's exciting. You can't guess the ending.
Tim	Can I borrow it?
Sally	Yes, you can have it next week.

4   Write answers to these questions in full sentences.

a) What is the book called? (**title**)
    It's _____

b) Who wrote it? (**author**)
    It's by _____

c) What type of book is it? (**type**)
    It's _____

d) What is it like? (**comments**)
    It's _____

Now read the beginning of the story.

Chapter One

The house was old. The windows were small and dark, like eyes. They looked unfriendly. The garden was overgrown.
    'Is this the right house?' thought Felicity. She looked uneasily at the name on the gate again. "Five Chimneys". It must be this one. It's the last house in the village.'
    Quickly, she opened the gate and walked along the path. It was slippery with rain. Drops of water fell from the wet trees.
    'Perhaps I don't want this job,' thought Felicity nervously. She remembered the advertisement in the newspaper:

Girl wanted November to work as assistant to writer. Live-in, country house. Must be 20-25, must type and drive. Please send references and recent photograph.

    She reached the door and knocked, softly at first and then more loudly. Footsteps sounded on the other side and the door opened slowly. The light fell on a girl. Felicity gasped.
    'No, it can't . . . I don't believe . . .'
    It was like a dream. The girl was like a twin sister. She looked exactly like Felicity.

Finding Words   5   Find words in the story

   a)   about the place:
            What did the house look like?
                     the windows
                     the garden
                     the path
                     the trees
   b)   about Felicity:
            How did Felicity look at the name?
                           open the gate?
                           think about the job?
                           knock on the door?

**Making
Sentences**

Now read this part of the story.

Felicity went into the bookshop. There was no-one there. A woman came out of a room at the back. She was tall and thin and she wore glasses.
   'I'm looking for Jane Malory,' said Felicity. The woman looked over the top of her glasses.
   'Jane Malory? I don't know anyone called Jane Malory,' she said.
   'But she came in here. I saw her.'
   'No,' said the woman. 'You can see there's no-one here. Is she a friend?'
   'She lives at Five Chimneys', said Felicity. 'Don't you know her?'
   'Five Chimneys?' said the woman. 'Oh, no. No-one lives there. The house is empty.'

6   Answer these questions with full sentences.

   a)   What type of shop does Felicity go into?
        She _____
   b)   Why?
        Because she sees _____
   c)   Who comes into the shop from a back room?
        A woman _____
   d)   What does the woman tell her?
        She doesn't know _____ and no-one _____
        The house _____

46

Organising Your Writing

7 Sally wrote a review of *The Secret of Five Chimneys*. Here are her notes. Write full sentences.

CHARACTERS
Felicity, girl, 23
Jane, mysterious writer

SETTING
old country house
winter, rainy & wet

EVENTS
At beginning of story – Felicity
answers job ad. – goes to house
– old, looks unfriendly – garden
overgrown.
She opens gate – walks along
path – slippery. Knocks at door –
door opens – sees girl – looks
like herself.

Then Jane disappears!

COMMENTS
Read book to find ending.
Good, exciting, can't guess ending

a) The main characters are Felicity, a twenty-three year-old girl, and Jane, a mysterious writer.

b) The story begins in _____
It is winter. The weather is _____

c) At the beginning of the story Felicity answers a job advertisement. She goes to the house. It is _____
She opens the gate and _____
She knocks _____
The door _____ and she sees _____
The girl _____

d) Then Jane disappears in a bookshop.

e) Read the story to find out the ending. It's very good. It's _____ and you can't _____

Writing It Out

8 Write about a book you know.

Title	What is the book called?
Author	Who wrote it?
Type	What type of book is it?
Characters	Who are the main characters?
Setting	Where and when does the story happen?
Events	What happens?
Comments	What's your opinion? Is it good/interesting/exciting/sad?

UNIT ELEVEN
We must get this story!

Finding Words

1 What do you know about newspapers? Match the words with their meanings.

interview	the person who takes pictures
cover	a piece of writing
editor	meet and talk to someone
reporter	the person who directs a newspaper
photographer	the first page of a paper
article	spoken or written information
statement	find out a story
front cover	the titles at the top of articles
headlines	the person who finds out stories

Learning New Words

Read the article and answer the questions.

SALTMARSH GAZETTE
ST MARY'S TO CLOSE

Two hurt in protest demonstration

Two people were hurt in a demonstration at St Mary's Hospital, Saltmarsh, this morning. About three hundred people met outside the main gates of the hospital at 7.45 this morning and walked up and down until 11 o'clock. They shouted and sang and carried large placards, – WE NEED ST MARY'S! STOP THE CLOSURE! and PATIENTS SAY NO TO HOSPITAL CLOSURE! They talked to doctors, nurses, office staff, . . . everyone going into the hospital.

An angry administrator drove his car at the demonstrators. Two were hurt. They are now inside the hospital.

Mrs Hilary Ward, chairperson of the Patients' Protest Group said, 'We hear the hospital is closing in November. But it isn't right. We need St Mary's. There isn't another hospital in this area. The nearest one is 30 miles away in Crichley.'

St Mary's is an old hospital. It needs new equipment and new buildings.

Is Mrs Ward's information correct? Nobody knows. The Hospital Administration is making a statement tomorrow.

2   Are these sentences true or false? Correct the false ones.

   a) People protested about the closure of St Mary's Hospital.
   b) St Mary's Hospital is in Crichley.
   c) The demonstration went on for about five hours.
   d) An angry administrator hit two demonstrators.
   e) Mrs Ward is chairperson of the Patients' Protest Group.
   f) The Hospital Administration made a statement.

3   Work with a friend. Ask and answer.

   a) Where is the article?
   b) What are the headlines?
   c) How many people demonstrated?
   d) What did the demonstrators do?
   e) What did Mrs Ward hear?
   f) Why mustn't the hospital close?
   g) Is St Mary's a modern hospital?
   h) When is the Hospital Administration making a statement?

4   Janet Frost is a reporter on the *Crichley Post*. Crichley is a small town near Saltmarsh. Janet is covering the St Mary's story.

Make notes.

Who can she interview?

Mrs Hilary Ward

What must she find out:
   about the hospital?

the number of patients

   about the Protest Group?

the number of members

   about the hospital staff?

49

Making Sentences

5 Jack Rivers is the Editor of the *Crichley Post*. Read this conversation and complete it with words from Exercise 1.

Jack Look at this _____ on the front cover of the Gazette.

News Editor The one about St Mary's Hospital and the protest?

Jack Yes. We must get this story. It's very important.

News Editor Yes, my telephone's ringing every two minutes. People in Crichley want to know about it.

Jack I want to see it on our _____ _____ tomorrow. And _____ 'St Mary's to Close! Is this what you want?' – or something like that. I want a _____ to go there at once.

News Editor Janet Frost is _____ it.

Jack Good. We need answers to these questions. How big is the hospital? How many patients has it got? How old is it? What do the doctors think? We need information about the Patients' Protest Group. We must talk to the Hospital Administration. I want lots of interviews and photographs. Remember to _____ the demonstrators in hospital.

6 What must the News Editor do? Make notes. Jack Rivers says:

a) I want headlines ST MARY'S TO CLOSE! or something like that.

Write headlines for the front page

b) I want a reporter to go there at once.

Send

c) We need answers to these questions.

Find out about

d) We need information about the Patients' Protest Group.

Get

e) We must talk to the Hospital Administration.

Talk

f) I want lots of interviews,

Interview

g) . . . and photographs.

Send

The News Editor rings Janet. What must she do?

News Editor	John here.
Janet	Oh, I'm just going to St Mary's.
John	Good. Take a photographer with you. We want lots of pictures.
Janet	Yes, I'm taking Eddy with me. I'm interviewing Henry Judson at three o'clock. He's in the Hospital Administration.
John	Good. We need lots of interviews. Ask for opinions. Talk to the doctors, nurses, patients, office staff, cleaners . . . everyone. And I want you to talk to the Patients' Protest Group. Find out all the facts, the numbers of members, its plans . . .
Janet	We need information about the hospital, too.
John	Yes, can you find out how old it is, the number of patients . . .
Janet	And what about the demonstrators?
John	We must have an interview with the two in hospital. Can you talk to them?

Writing It Out   7 Here are Janet's notes. Complete them.

```
a) Take Eddy with me
b) Get
c) See
d) Interview
e) Ask
f) Talk
g) Find out
h) Get
i) Find out
j) Interview
```

UNIT TWELVE
Eighteen is too young to vote!

Evening Gazette
FOURTEEN-YEAR-OLD CRIMINALS

Evening Gazette
Eighteen is too young to vote!

YOUNG PEOPLE SAY NO TO WORK
Evening Gazette

Evening Gazette
ALCOHOLICS UNDER EIGHTEEN
Do our young people drink too much?

What do you think?

Is eighteen too young to vote?
Do you think young people don't want to work?

What do you know?

Are many teenagers alcoholics in your country?
Are there many young criminals?

Mr Lewis wrote to the
Evening Gazette.
Read his letter and
do the exercises.

> 24 Acacia Drive,
> Greenstead
>
> 6 May
>
> Dear Sir,
>
> (1) I read all of your articles about young people today. (2) I think young people are terrible. (3) They don't get jobs because they don't pass their exams. (4) I know how lazy they are. (5) The children in my street sit on the wall outside my house and smoke. (6) They play very loud music on their radios and make a terrible noise. (7) I shout at them but they just laugh at me.
>
> (8) My neighbour is an old lady. (9) She is afraid to go out because she says teenagers today frighten old people and steal their money.
>
> (10) The children on my estate broke two of my windows and wrote things on the wall in white paint.
>
> (11) And these young people can vote in an election at eighteen. It's all wrong!
>
> Yours faithfully
>
> M.S. Lewis

Working With Sentences

1 Where can you put these sentences in the letter.

I believe you're right.	They don't work hard at school.
They leave ugly litter in my garden.	I hope the police catch them.

2 Write answers to these questions:

a) Why does Mr Lewis think young people don't get jobs?
b) What do the children in his street do?
c) Why is his neighbour afraid to go out?
d) What did the children on his estate do?
e) What can young people do at eighteen?
f) Does he think this is right?

Learning New Words

3 Complete each sentence with an adjective. Write the number in the box.

a) ☐   I can't believe it's right. It must be ＿＿＿

b) ☐   That boy is very ＿＿＿ . He never does any work.

c) ☐   I like listening to soft music. That record's too ＿＿＿

d) ☐   Caroline was ＿＿＿ to show her parents
e) ☐   her ＿＿＿ exam results.

i	lazy

iii	loud

v	afraid

ii	terrible

iv	wrong

Making Sentences

4 Look at this sentence from the letter.

They don't get jobs *because* they don't pass their exams.

Make six sentences from the table.

The caretaker was angry You mustn't smoke She wrote to the newspaper The politician spoke loudly The old lady rang the police We voted for him	because	she wanted to give her opinion. it's very bad for you. she was afraid. the children broke all the windows. he wanted everyone to hear him. he understands our problems.

5 Look at these opinions. What do you think? Write five things.

   a) I think _____
   b) They _____
   c) I believe _____
   d) I say _____
   e) I know _____

I'm eighteen. I have a job. I pay taxes. I drive a car. I can get married. I want to vote too.

My children are very good. They like pop music but they play it in their own room. They help in the house.

Most young people are very kind. They like loud music that's not bad, I do, too.

They are bored. There's nothing interesting here, no clubs, no sports. They have nothing to do.

A lot of young people work very hard at school. They get good jobs.

I passed all my examinations but I can't get a job. There are no jobs here. Older people don't understand. They think I'm lazy.

A lot of teenagers are very kind. They belong to Community Work Groups. They help old people.

6   Karen is being interviewed on a radio programme. Make the interview by numbering each speech.

☐ Some old people say they are afraid to go out.

☐ You say 'Most young people' . . .

[1] Karen, what do you think about voting at eighteen?

☐ Was it easy to get a job?

☐ Yes, I know. There are some teenage criminals and there are some teenage alcoholics . . . but I think they need help.

☐ I'm eighteen. I can vote in the election this year. I believe it's right. I'm married, I've got a job, I pay taxes. I want to vote.

☐ Yes, of course there are some lazy ones. There are some teenagers who break windows. There are some who make a lot of noise but on my estate a lot of young people do community work. They help old people.

☐ No, it isn't easy to get a job. Lots of young people work very hard at school but there are no jobs. I went to thirty interviews. Most young people aren't lazy.

Organising Your Writing

7   Look at the points **against** young people. Make points **for** them. Use Karen's opinions.

a) These young people can vote in an election at eighteen. It's all wrong!

_I think ____

b) They don't get jobs because they don't pass their exams. They don't work hard at school.

_Lots of____

c) The children on my estate broke two of my windows and wrote on the garden wall.

_Of course there are ____

d) Most young people drink too much.

_There are ____

f) They frighten old people and steal their money.

_There are ____ but ____

Writing It Out

8   Now write a letter from Karen to the *Evening Gazette*. Begin like this:

> 14 Magnolia Avenue
> Greenstead
>
> 9 May
>
> Dear Sir
> I read all your articles about young people today and I read the letter from M.S. Lewis. I think he's wrong ____

Consolidation

1 Everyone likes him!

Describing a person

1 Vocabulary*

Looks	Clothes	Personality
tall	casual	lively
short	smart	quiet
slim	fashionable	thoughtful
thin	unfashionable	cheerful
plump	modern	miserable
fat	unusual	sympathetic
dark ⎫	colourful	serious
fair ⎬ hair		honest
brown	jeans	gentle
red ⎭	jacket	kind
short	dress	funny
long ⎫	skirt	
curly ⎬ hair	jumper	
wavy		
straight ⎭		
blue ⎫		
green ⎬ eyes		
brown		
grey ⎭		
beard		
moustache		
glasses		

* The vocabulary lists in this section may contain some words not in the unit, but these are relevant and help to expand vocabulary.

2 Something to do for yourself

Write a description of this girl. Use your imagination.

56

2 Is it near the sea?
Describing a place

1 Vocabulary

Things in a house	Services	Describing a house	Things to do
living room kitchen bedrooms breakfast corner balcony bathroom double bed single bed open fire shower room dining room patio	central heating payphone colour TV garage private parking barbecue	detached large beautifully-furnished pretty modernised lovely comfortable modern style	cycling sailing horse-riding tennis swimming touring fishing picnics

2 Something to do for yourself

Where are you going for your next holiday? Write a letter about it.

3 He never gets up early
Describing activities

1 Vocabulary

When	How often	Activities	

in the summer
in the winter
on Saturday
  evenings
on Sunday
  mornings
on weekday
  evenings
	never
	rarely
	sometimes
	often
	always
		go the cinema
		visit friends
		watch TV
		go for a walk
		watch football
		read a newspaper
		stay at home
		go to a party
		go skiing
			go swimming
			get up early
			go fishing
			read a book
			play football
			go skating
			go for a walk
			go sailing
			play ice-hockey

2 Something to do for yourself

a) Complete this description of Mrs Green.

In the winter Mrs Green often _____ . She sometimes _____ TV and she
sometimes _____ friends. In the summer she sometimes _____ sailing with her
husband and she _____ goes for a walk with the dog. She rarely goes swimming
because she _____ like swimming. On Saturday evenings she often _____ or she
_____ at home. On Sunday mornings she _____ or she cooks dinner for the
family. On weekday evenings she sometimes _____ to French classes or
sometimes she _____

b) Now write a description of your other friend. Use the notes on page 17.

4 Come to my party!
Writing instructions

1 Vocabulary

Transport	Culture	Services	Shops	Entertainment and Sport
railway station bus station bus stop car park	library theatre art gallery museum	church school café bank hospital health centre	supermarket post office baker's greengrocer's butcher's newsagent's	pub club cinema tennis courts sports hall football pitch swimming pool

2 Something to do for yourself

You are having a party. Invite a friend and write a letter. Write directions to your house.

5 Are you a new student?
Writing a dialogue

1 Vocabulary

Information about people	Study words	Clubs and Societies	Adjectives about work/study

name
age
nationality
country of
  origin
address
study details
work details
ambition
feelings about
  job
interests
	fresher
	part-time
	full-time
	Secretarial
	  Studies
	Business
	  Studies
	Tourism
	Hotel Reception
	  and Catering
	Photography
	Economics
		Swimming Club
		Mountaineering Club
		Tennis Club
		Industrial Society
		Photography Club
		Athletics Association
		Music Society
			interesting
			creative
			practical
			satisfying
			useful
			hard

2 Something to do for yourself

Write a dialogue between Ana and one of the other students.

6 Don't leave anything behind!
Persuading people to do things

1 Vocabulary

Phrases for writing rules	The hostel	Adjectives	Activities in a hostel
Please remember to . . .	dormitory	late	do the washing up
Always . . .	washroom	tidy	peel the potatoes
You must . . .	common room	clean	cook in the kitchen
You mustn't . . .	kitchen	angry	help with the housework
Don't . . .	warden	simple	use a sleeping bag
Please help to . . .	hosteller	cheap	talk for hours
Don't forget to . . .	rules	comfortable	waste food
Make sure . . .	sleeping bag	friendly	change your shoes
	housebook		make your bed
			make a noise
			keep the dormitory tidy
			set the tables
			clear the tables
			be quiet

2 Something to do for yourself

Does your office, workplace, home, school or college have rules? Make a list.

7 West Africa welcomes the Pope
Writing a report

1 Vocabulary

Verbs-past simple tense

Regular	Irregular
landed	sang
welcomed	beat
danced	met
listened	left
addressed	flew
blessed	made
stayed	drove
asked	brought
finished	

2 Something to do for yourself

Look in a newspaper for information about a visit by a famous person. Make a diary of events. Write a summary of the visit.

8 A day out
Writing an account

1 Vocabulary

Verbs (past simple)	Things to do	Places	When?
met	a tour	a zoo	First of all . . .
left	a picnic	a museum	Next . . .
took	a visit	a sailing ship	At . . . o'clock
went	a trip	a palace	Then . . .
looked	a walk	a tower	In the afternoon . . .
saw	a performance	a cathedral	After that . . .
drove			In the evening . . .
had			
travelled			
missed			

2 Something to do for yourself

Think about a trip you took recently. Write an account of it.

9 I prefer Biology to Maths
Discussing things

1 Vocabulary

Subjects	Adjectives	Activities	Verbs to express likes, dislikes and preferences
Music	main	study	like
English Literature	difficult	read	don't like
French	different	play	prefer
German	good	visit	like better than
Italian	bad	paint	
Biology	careless	sing	
Zoology	interesting		
Chemistry	favourite		
Physics	intelligent		
Medicine	kind		
Technical Drawing	important		
Woodwork			
Mechanics			
History			
Cookery			

2	Something to do for yourself	Here is some information about Mercedes. Write a letter from Mercedes to her penfriend.

College:	Commercial College
Main subjects:	Business Studies, Typing, Shorthand
Other subjects:	French, English
Interests:	Dancing, Music Club

10 The Secret of Five Chimneys
Writing a review

1 Vocabulary

Types of book	Reviewing a book	Writing a mystery story adjectives	adverbs
a biography	title	old	uneasily
a love story	author	small	quickly
a historical novel	type	dark	slowly
a detective story	characters	unfriendly	softly
a thriller	setting	overgrown	loudly
a mystery story	events	slippery	nervously
a war book	comments	wet	
a travel book			

2	Something to do for yourself	Practise reading your review out loud and read it to your class.

11 We must get this story!
Working with information

1 Vocabulary

Newspaper vocabulary	Hospital vocabulary	Protest vocabulary	Verbs for planning
interview (vb)	patients	protests (vb)	write
cover (vb)	doctors	protest group	send
editor	nurses	members	find out
reporter	office staff	demonstration	get
photographer	administrator	demonstrators	talk to
article	administration	demonstrate (vb)	ask for
statement	equipment	placards	tell (someone) to (do
front cover	buildings		something)
headlines	gates		take
	closure		see
			interview

2 Something to do for yourself   What are you doing tomorrow? Plan your day. Make a list.

12 Eighteen is too young to vote!
Giving opinions

1 Vocabulary

Verbs to give opinions	Other verbs	Nouns	Adjectives
think	frighten	teenagers	young, old
believe	steal	alcoholics	good, bad
hope	smoke	exams	loud, soft
say	make a noise	neighbour	lazy
know	break	paint	terrible
	write	litter	ugly
	pass exams	caretaker	afraid
	work hard	politician	wrong, right
	catch	election	angry
	leave litter	estate	kind
	give your opinion		bored
	understand a problem		interesting
			angry

2 Something to do for yourself   Write a letter to the *Evening Gazette*. Give <u>your</u> opinions about young people.

Answers to closed exercises

1 Everyone likes him!

5   a) ii   b) iv   c) v   d) iii   e) i

2 Is it near the sea?

1   attractive   sunny   comfortable   open   modernised   single
historic   colour

3   a) false   b) false   c) false   d) false   e) true
f) true   g) false   h) false

3 He never gets up early.

7   a) true   b) false   c) false   d) false   e) false
f) true

4 Come to my party!

1   A church   B school   C station   D café
E library   F farm   G pub   H telephone box
I village pond

4   to   from   opposite   next to   at   in   around
into   along   over   by   on

6   a) Avenue   b) Terrace   c) Road
d) Crescent   e) Gardens   f) Street

6 Don't leave anything behind!

1   simple   member   dormitories   meals   kitchen
hosteller   housework   warden   rules

7 West Africa welcomes the Pope

3   left   made   met/welcomed   listened   flew   sang
danced   drove/rode   blessed   flew   stayed

4   a) false   b) false   c) false   d) true   e) true

5   on   at   in   in   the evening   next   to
for one day

8 A day out

1   trip   Saturday   20th   Are   much   Can   two
     groups   boat   Do   don't   the   zoo   write/put

3   a) true   b) false   c) true   d) true
    e) false   f) true   g) false   h) true
    i) false   j) true

9 I prefer Biology to Maths

1   and   but   and   because   and   because   and
    because   and   and

2   a) and   b) and/but   c) but   d) but
    e) because   f) but   g) because   h) but

3   a) viii   b) ix   c) ii   d) vi/iii   e) iii/vi
    f) i   g) vii   h) iv   i) v

11 We must get this story!

2   a) true   b) false   c) false   d) false
    e) true   f) false

5   article   front cover   headline   reporter   covering
    interview

12 Eighteen is too young to vote!

3   a) iv   b) i   c) iii   d) v   e) ii